Martin Luther King Jr. Day

ABDO
Publishing Company

A Buddy Book
by
Julie Murray

Published by ABDO Publishing Company, 4940 Viking Drive, Edina, Minnesota 55435.

Copyright © 2005 by Abdo Consulting Group, Inc. International copyrights reserved in all countries. No part of this book may be reproduced in any form without written permission from the publisher. Buddy Books™ is a trademark and logo of ABDO Publishing Company.

Printed in the United States.

Edited by: Sarah Tieck
Contributing Editor: Michael P. Goecke
Graphic Design: Denise Esner
Image Research: Deborah Coldiron, Maria Hosley
Photographs: Corel, Hulton Archives, Image 100

Library of Congress Cataloging-in-Publication Data

Murray, Julie, 1969-
  Martin Luther King, Jr. Day / Julie Murray.
     p. cm. — (Holidays)
  Includes index.
  Contents: A national holiday — A country divided — Martin Luther King Jr. — The bus boycott — The civil rights movement — I have a dream — A sad day in America — The making of a holiday — Celebrations today.
  ISBN 1-59197-589-1
     1. Martin Luther King, Jr., Day—Juvenile literature. 2. King, Martin Luther, Jr.,
  1929–1968 —Juvenile literature. [1. Martin Luther King, Jr., Day. 2. King, Martin Luther, Jr., 1929–1968. 3. Civil rights workers. 4. Holidays.] I. Title.

E185.97.K5M866 2004
23'.092—dc23
                                                            2003063806

Table of Contents

What Is Martin Luther King Jr. Day?

Martin Luther King Jr. Day celebrates a man's life and work. Martin Luther King Jr. was the leader of the **civil rights movement**. He fought for equal rights for people. His work helped bring an end to **segregation**.

Martin Luther King Jr. was a minister and civil rights leader.

Martin Luther King Jr. Day is a national **holiday** in the United States. It is celebrated on the third Monday of January each year. Most schools, banks, and government offices are closed on this day.

Schools teach children about Martin Luther King Jr.'s life.

Fighting For Civil Rights

Martin Luther King Jr. was the leader of the **civil rights movement**. He fought for **equality** for African Americans and all people in the United States. He won a Nobel Peace Prize for his work.

Martin Luther King Jr. receives the Nobel Peace Prize in Oslo, Norway.

Martin Luther King Jr. did not want people to fight. In 1957, he became the leader of the Southern Christian Leadership Conference. This group worked for **civil rights**. They **protested** in peaceful ways. They carried banners, listened to speeches, held protests, and sang songs.

Martin Luther King Jr. and others march for civil rights in Alabama.

Many people did not like what Martin Luther King Jr. said about **civil rights**. They did not think people with different skin colors were equal to white people.

Peaceful Ways

Martin Luther King Jr. and his followers **protested** in peaceful ways. King learned about this from Mohandas Gandhi.

In 1959, Martin Luther King Jr. went to India to meet Gandhi. Gandhi taught King about peaceful protest. King used Gandhi's methods to fight for equal rights.

Mohandas Gandhi used peaceful protest to help bring equal rights to Africa and India.

The Making Of A Holiday

After Martin Luther King Jr. died in 1968, people wanted to honor him. They tried to make his birthday a **holiday**. Congress did not make this a law. Still, many states honored King on January 15.

In 1983, President Ronald Reagan made a national holiday. The third Monday of January became Martin Luther King Jr. Day.

Postage stamps honor
Martin Luther King Jr.

The first official celebration of Martin Luther King Jr. Day was Monday, January 20, 1986. This was the first federal **holiday** to honor an African American.

I Have A Dream

Martin Luther King Jr. is famous for his "I Have a Dream" speech. He gave this speech at the Lincoln Memorial on August 28, 1963. More than 250,000 people marched to Washington, D.C., to show their support.

Martin Luther King Jr. talks to the crowd during the March on Washington.

"I Have A Dream" is about Martin Luther King Jr.'s ideas for America's future. The following is a passage from this famous speech:

"... I have a dream that my four little children will one day live in a nation where they will not be judged by the color of their skin but by the content of their character ..."

Celebrations Today

Today, people around the world celebrate Martin Luther King Jr. Day. They honor him in many different ways. Some cities in the United States have special Martin Luther King Jr. Day celebrations.

Some people celebrate Martin Luther King Jr. Day with parades.

The Life Of A Leader

January 15, 1929—Martin Luther King Jr. was born in Atlanta, Georgia.

January 25, 1948—He was **ordained** in the Baptist ministry. His father was a minister, too.

June 18, 1953—Martin Luther King Jr. married Coretta Scott.

October 1954—Martin Luther King Jr. began preaching at the Dexter Avenue Church in Montgomery, Alabama.

December 1, 1955—An African-American woman named Rosa Parks refused to give up her seat on a bus. King organized a boycott of this bus company.

February 1959—Martin Luther King Jr. visited a man named Mohandas Gandhi in India. Gandhi taught him about **protesting** in a peaceful way.

August 28, 1963—King gave his "I Have a Dream" speech in Washington, D.C.

December 10, 1964—Martin Luther King Jr. received the Nobel Peace Prize.

February 9, 1965—King met President Lyndon B. Johnson. They talked about voting rights for African Americans.

April 4, 1968—James Earl Ray shot and killed Martin Luther King Jr. in Memphis, Tennessee.

Index